THE
FULFILLMENT
PRINCIPLE

THE FULFILLMENT PRINCIPLE

*Experiencing
a Life of Pure Joy
and Fulfillment*

BOB WESTFALL

LEAFWOOD
PUBLISHERS

THE FULFILLMENT PRINCIPLE
Experiencing a Life of Pure Joy and Fulfillment

Copyright 2011 by Bob Westfall

ISBN 978-0-89112-287-6
LCCN 2011024916

Printed in the United States of America

Scripture quotations, unless otherwise noted, are taken from the New American Standard Bible®, Copyright © 1960, 1962, 1963, 1968, 1971, 1972, 1973, 1975, 1977, 1995 by The Lockman Foundation. Used by permission. Scripture quotations noted NIV are taken from the HOLY BIBLE, NEW INTERNATIONAL VERSION®. Copyright © 1973, 1978, 1984 Biblica. Used by permission of Zondervan. All rights reserved. Scripture quotations noted ESV are from The Holy Bible, English Standard Version® (ESV®), copyright © 2001 by Crossway, a publishing ministry of Good News Publishers. Used by permission. All rights reserved.

LIBRARY OF CONGRESS CATALOGING-IN-PUBLICATION DATA
Westfall, Bob.
 The fulfillment principle : experiencing a life of pure joy and fulfillment / Bob Westfall.
     p. cm.
  ISBN 978-0-89112-287-6
  1. Self-realization--Religious aspects--Christianity. 2. Joy--Religious aspects--Christianity.
I. Title.
  BV4598.2.W45 2011
  248.4--dc23
                                                                        2011024916

Cover design by Thinkpen Design, LLC
Interior text design by Sandy Armstrong

Leafwood Publishers • 1626 Campus Court • Abilene, Texas 79601

1-877-816-4455 toll free

For current information about all Leafwood titles, visit our website:
www.leafwoodpublishers.com

               11 12 13 14 15 16 / 7 6 5 4 3 2 1

*To my adorable wife Kim for doing life with me
and for the inspiration to write this book.*

*To Lauren Gaither for her editorial skill
and dogged determination,
and to my friend Ceston Mapes
—without your expertise this would not
have become a reality.*

*Finally, to my children
Brittni, Jessica, Austin, and Alyssa—
you have been so patient with me as
I have invested my talent for God's Kingdom.*

CONTENTS

Foreword

by Bruce Wilkinson

We make a living by what we get,
but we make a life by what we give.

— Winston Churchill

W hy is it that joy seems to sag easily under the pressure-beams of life? Why is joy so quick to unravel when the stress of life pulls tightly around us? Could it be that this symptom is trying to whisper to us of a deeper problem—telling us that we've missed something along the way? Is it truly possible to find the kind of joy that stretches its roots deep into the soil of our lives? Fixed and unmoving? Tenacious joy . . . *pure joy?*

This pure joy that *The Fulfillment Principle* speaks of lies at the heart of the gospel story. The prophet

Isaiah foretold the coming joy of God's people: ". . . everlasting *joy* shall be upon their heads; they shall obtain gladness and *joy*, and sorrow and sighing shall flee away" (Isa. 35:10 ESV).

In the midst of intimate talk with his disciples, Christ laid bare this same hope for us: ". . . these things I have spoken to you, that my joy may be in you, *and that your joy may be full*" (John 15:11 ESV, emphasis mine). Christ, God become flesh, wants our joy to be *full*—filled to the brim, bursting at the seams. In these ancient and living words, we find a profound announcement: our hearing and understanding of His truth directly influences our capacity for joy. The question remains, subtle and simple, if our joy is forever bound up in him, how do we go about finding this lasting fulfillment . . . this joy-*full*-ness?

The book you hold in your hands—written with straightforward, inviting candor—is a wonderful mingling of instruction and encouragement. It will find you wherever you are on the path to joy, meet you there, continue on the journey with you, and lend some remarkable energy and inspiration along the way. Whether your joy has been wearied from circumstances, disappointments, waylaid dreams—or if you are simply searching for a way to expand the broad shoulders of already-present joy in your life— this book is for you.

The Fulfillment Principle, by Bob Westfall, will help you find and examine the pulse of joy in your life and open your eyes to new possibilities for joy within your reach. The kind of joy that reorients our perspectives, embraces life, and wakes up the world.

Bob has been a close friend of mine for many years—a companion on this journey to seek the heart of Christ as we sink our teeth into the deep and lasting joy he offers. *The Fulfillment Principle* is comprised of inspirational and biblical instruction on how to discover this richer life, what brings true joy, how to find it, and how to make it grow for a lifetime.

Bob understands the significance of purpose-driven joy and serves as a worthy guide and co-journeyer. I have personally watched his ministry, influence, and joy expand as he has integrated the truth he presents within these pages. I have known Bob throughout his leadership role as Senior Vice President of Walk Thru the Bible, and in his more recent focus of impacting dozens of major Christian organizations through raising more than $220 million in a very short time. His life bears witness to the success and joy of serving Christ fully by maximizing all available resources. *The Fulfillment Principle* is a motivational meditation upon the true claims of Christ's *Parable of the Talents*. It studies the words in their original first-century context, and then explores the principle's impact upon us today—how it affects our joy, our sense of meaning, and our direction.

I hope your heart stirs and joy billows up as you read the mingling of Christ's ancient words and Bob's contemporary voice of encouragement. May you discover the joyful freedom of serving Christ—the good Master, the reigning King—with all He has given you. May the clarity you gain from this book bring about new and lasting fullness, and as your joy grows, let it surround your life and work with a rich anticipation of the coming words of Christ, "Well done, faithful one . . . *Enter into my joy."*

www.BruceWilkinson.com
www.Facebook.com/LastingLifeChange

1

EXPERIENCING
TRUE JOY

God wants you to "enter in"

*It is vanity to love that which passeth away,
and not to hasten where eternal joy abideth.*

— *The Imitation of Christ* 1:4, Thomas á Kempis

There's something you want, we all want. In fact, our hearts ache for it. Some of us realize it sooner than others. Unfortunately, some of us never realize it at all.

It's joy. It's fulfillment.

It's a pleasure and contentment and peace—an unending spring of living water—that runs deep within our very being.

Do you have it?

Books have been written about going from "good to great" and from "success to significance." But this little book is different. It's intentionally written *not* to give you a temporary high or take you on a mountain-top experience, only to let you fall back to reality again, unchanged, trying in your flesh to cling to the concepts you read in some manual.

The 100-proof fulfillment principle conveyed through the stories and scriptures in this book is bulletproof. Fears arise, uncertainty looms, storms hit, but the joy is there, inside you—a rock that can't be rolled, a fire that can't be quenched, a contentment that can't be contaminated.

Many people have heard the story of the talents in the Bible. A man—who is a picture of Jesus—is about to go on a journey. Before he leaves, he calls his servants—a picture of us—and doles out his possessions to them. One servant is given five talents, one is given two talents, another is given one talent.

Before I get further into the details of the parable, however, allow me to jump to a segment of the story that most people overlook. I did, until the winter of 2001 when a life-changing nugget from this tale hit me like a semi-truck sent from heaven, proverbially altering the way I live and move and have my being.

You see, at the time I was experiencing some incredible personal challenges with my life feeling unfulfilled. I was successful at work, but feeling as though I had missed my mark and my calling.

The words I'm referring to—the ones that changed the landscape of my life once and for all—are those of the man who went on the journey, the man who represents Jesus in the parable.

When that man returns from his long trip, he sees that the men who were given five talents and two talents had invested the money, each making double what he'd left them. In response, the master says: "'Well done, good and faithful slave; you were faithful with a few things, I will put you in charge of many things, *enter into the joy of your master*'" (Matt. 25:21, emphasis mine).

Hold it right there.

"Enter into the joy of your master?"

Where did that come from?

Everyone knows the part that says, "Well done, good and faithful slave." And some people know about the, "You were faithful with a few things, I will put you in charge of many things." But how many people realize that in this oft-repeated text, the creator of the universe hands his children a clear, concise blueprint for pure joy?

And we're talking about you and me, entering in to *his* joy—a joy unspeakable and unending—right now.

Not tomorrow.

Not next week or month.

But today.

Not only pastors or missionaries.

Not only scholars and saints.

But you and me. School teachers and business people, housewives and home school moms, mechanics and mill workers, computer geeks and career women.

How many people realize that in this oft-repeated text, the creator of the universe hands his children a clear, concise blueprint for pure joy?

How do you get to that place where you can almost see God smiling as he whispers those words: "Enter into the joy of your master"?

Perhaps the easiest way to get you there is by going in the opposite direction. . . .

Discussion Questions

1) Do you believe God wants you to have joy here on earth?

2) Read the parable of the talents in Mathew 25: 14-30. What, in your opinion, is the main overall message in this passage?

3) In the parable of the talents, what do you think the Master means when he says, "Enter into the joy of your Master?" Is it meant for you, today? How do you attain it?

4) Are you fulfilled in your current work or occupation?

2

THE KEY
TO YOUR JOY

It may be right under your nose

Don't ask yourself what the world needs.
Ask yourself what makes you come alive,
and then go do that.
Because what the world needs is people
who have come alive.

— Reverend Howard Thurman

A well-known pastor friend knew I was traveling to the Dallas-Fort Worth area and asked if I would meet with his son, who was in seminary there. "He's really down right now," my friend said. "He needs some advice and encouragement. And he respects you."

I agreed and set up a time to meet.

After small talk over breakfast, I said to the young man, "Tell me how it's going?"

"Terrible. Just awful," the young man said. "Here I am a seminary student and I feel like God has called me to be the senior pastor of a church. I'm so frustrated. I know I'm supposed to be a senior pastor."

"Hold on a second," I said. "You're still in school. You're working toward your degree. I'm sure God still has some things he wants to show you."

The young man wrung his hands and moved uncomfortably in his chair. No, he was ready to pastor. It was straight to the top for him.

"Tell me what you're doing today, besides school?" I asked.

"I've got to pay for seminary, so I cut grass. I've formed a small landscape company. Two guys work for me."

"Oh? Tell me the spiritual condition of the two guys who work for you?"

He squinted. "I have no idea . . . I mean, we cut grass."

"Okay, tell me what you're doing in church."

"Well, I'm an associate pastor and I teach a Sunday school class."

"How many people are in the class?"

"Just two couples right now. They have families."

"And what's the spiritual condition of those two couples?"

He ran a hand through his hair and shook his head. "I really don't think they're that spiritual. They're not committed. A lot of times they don't show up. It's been a real battle . . . like pulling teeth."

I knew what was happening. As an outsider, it was clear as day to me. But he couldn't see it. Perhaps he didn't want to.

"What I'd like you to do is take a look back to the parable of the talents," I said, "and imagine for a moment that you have two talents God has entrusted to you: the couples in your Sunday school class and the workers in your landscape business."

He stared at me blankly.

"Now I'm going to ask you what the master asks the servants in the parable. 'I've entrusted two talents to you. What have you done with them?'"

I'm telling you, I watched the blood drain from the young man's face.

Silence fell over our table.

"Nothing," was all he could muster.

God's word had found its way to the core of his being.

"Remember the promise?" I asked. "Once the slave said, 'Master, you entrusted to me two talents; see, I have gained two more talents.' His master said to him, 'Well done, good and faithful slave.' Of course, everybody wants to hear those words. But let's think about what the master says next: 'You were faithful with a few things, I will put you in charge of many things; enter into the joy of your master.'

"What your actions say to me is that the two guys who work for you and the two couples in your Sunday school class are not important to you," I said. "What's important to you is *your dream* to be a senior pastor. But what God wants you to do is not forsake the two

*When you show that you value the talents he's already given you, **then** he can trust you with more—and you can enter into his joy.*

talents he's given you. In other words, the end does not justify the means."

I've seen the scenario a million times. A pastor wants a mega-ministry or a global outreach. He's gone days on end, slaving away at his dream, up late and out early. Meanwhile, his wife and children are at home, dying on the vine.

"What God's looking for," I told the young man, "is faithfulness in the little things, the things that may not seem important to you. Are you going to invest in that which God has given you today, the things you may not have even noticed, but the things that, I can assure you, matter to him? When you show that you value the talents he's already given you, *then* he can trust you with more—and you can enter into his joy."

The young man's father phoned me that evening.

"What did you do to my son?"

"Only what we talked about," I said. "I gave him some advice and encouraged him."

"Well, he listened to you!"

Now, the question is, are you listening to God as he reveals the talents he's placed directly under your nose?

Discussion Questions

1) Have you ever felt as if God was leading you to pursue a certain calling?

2) Are you pursuing that calling? Why or why not?

3) If you are not pursing that "calling" or have not received one, what are you doing today and is it significant to God?

4) Discuss the statement that God has you right where he wants you, even though you might think you should be someplace else.

5) Pride can sometimes get in the way of accomplishing the things God wants us to accomplish. Has this ever been true for you?

6) Have you been faithful "in the little things?" Be honest and discuss.

3

YOUR VISION: LIKE NO OTHER

The God who gives us dreams, makes them come true

To find out what one is fitted to do, and to secure an opportunity to do it, is the key to happiness.

—John Dewey

The word "talent" spoken of in the parable of the talents (Matt. 25:14-30) is a measure of weight and, in this usage, means "money." As in many of Christ's parables, however, the story contains multiple layers of meaning and wisdom.

"For it is just like a man about to go on a journey, who called his own slaves, and entrusted his possessions to them. To one he gave five talents, to another, two, and to another, one, *each according to his own ability;* and he went on his journey" (Matt. 25:14, 15, emphasis mine).

Notice that God gives us something of his to invest—according to our ability. Who gave us our ability?

God.

So, although God may have given you five talents and me two and someone else one, he views us each the same. Just because you have more does not mean God views you as more valuable or important. Indeed, God sees us all as equal; he values us the same. And what he truly values most is the way you and I steward the talents he's entrusted into our lives. How do we invest those talents? Are we fruitful? Do we get a good return on the deposit he's made in our lives? Instead of the popular term, "return on investment (ROI)," I've coined it, "return on talent (ROT)."

What talent—be it treasure or ability or passion or skill—has God entrusted to you today? It might be a flock of a thousand church members, it may be twins in diapers. It might be an up-and-coming ad agency of ten people, or a rescue unit in which you provide a home for lost animals. You may be a mother of five or

---

*What has God entrusted to you—according to your
unique ability? What passion has he woven into
your heart, and only your heart?*

---

a single dad. You may be a meter reader, a steel worker,
or the CEO of a multi-million dollar company.

The question is still the same.

What has God entrusted to you—according to
your unique ability?

What passion has he woven into your heart, and
only your heart?

Ask Sean Lambert, the founder and president of
Youth With A Mission San Diego/Baja. Youth With
A Mission (YWAM) is a large international, inter-
denominational movement started in 1960 by Loren
Cunningham with the theme of knowing God and
making him known.

While on a mission trip in Tijuana, Mexico, in May
of 1990, Sean and his daughter, Andrea, joined a team
of fifteen people to build a house for a poverty-stricken

family. When the house was complete and the family moved in, Andrea pointed out another poor family living in an old abandoned bus adjacent to the new Home of Hope being built and said, "Daddy, are you going to build a house for that family too? What about the family living in the bus, are you going to build them a house?"

Andrea's words moved Sean to build a second house and Homes of Hope was born (ywamsdb.org). Starting with this single house in Tijuana, Mexico, Homes of Hope has now built 3,482 homes for poor families in ten different nations. One of the "talents" knitted into Sean's make-up is his love and compassion for the poor. He was faithful with the one house God sent him to build and so God put him in charge of many. Today, Homes of Hope impacts poor and needy families in five key areas: economic, educational, health, social and emotional, and spiritual.

Sean is an excellent example of someone who took small, simple steps in obeying God, entering into all God wanted to do in and through his life in a ministry that is now impacting ten other nations . . . and growing!

Now, back to you.

What abilities has God given you, and what "talents" has he instilled in you that coincide with your abilities? What has he put on *your* heart and *only your heart*? In essence, what has God built you, and only you, to accomplish?

There is a young man in Arizona by the name of Austin Gutwein who, at the ripe old age of ten, saw a video about a girl in Africa who lost her parents to HIV/AIDS and it gripped his heart. He learned that 5,700 children are orphaned each day because of HIV/AIDS, and that fifteen million children have already lost one or both parents to the disease.

"That hit me hard," recalls Austin, now sixteen. "I felt God calling me to go do something about it. I just kept thinking about it and kept thinking about it, and I finally decided, 'You know what? I've just got to go out and do something.'"

A friend suggested Austin use his favorite sport, basketball, to make a difference. What an amazing prophetic word that turned out to be! Remember, at the time Austin was just ten years old. Do you know what he did? He got some friends involved in shooting free-throws to raise money for those children in

Africa who had been orphaned as a result of the HIV/ AIDS pandemic.

Then something miraculous happened. God used the faith of that little kid from Arizona and he birthed Hoops of Hope (www.hoopsofhope.org), which has since become the world's largest free-throw marathon. Dozens upon dozens of schools, churches, organizations, and kids like Austin, have hosted shoot-a-thons around the world to raise money to help orphans in Africa.

Some 40,000 children have participated in Hoops of Hope, raising more than $2.5 million and allowing the organization to build a school in Zambia where there was no school for seventy miles. Not only that, Hoops of Hope has partnered with World Vision to build four dormitories for students of the school, two medical clinics, a computer lab, and more.

Just look what God did through one willing, compassionate boy.

2004

Raised $3,000 to care for eight orphan children.

2005

Raised $35,000 to care for a hundred orphan children.

2006

Raised $85,000 to help build the Jonathan Sim Legacy School in Twachiyanda, Zambia. Now, a thousand children are able to attend school.

2007

Raised $211,000 and built a medical testing lab/clinic in Sinazongwe, Zambia. This clinic will keep parents alive and prevent children from becoming orphans. It is said the clinic will save an entire generation.

2008

Raised $405,000 which was used as follows:

- $47,000 to complete the construction of the lab in Sinazongwe.
- $155,000 to build a completed water system in Kenya.

- $202,000 towards the building of a second clinic in Chilala, Zambia.

2009

Raised $611,000 which was used as follows:

- $198,000 to build dormitories for 280 children at the Jonathan Sim School in Twachiyanda.
- $82,000 to build two Orphan Hope Centers in Swaziland.
- $120,000 to complete the funding of the Chilala clinic.
- $41,000 to provide 250 bicycles and 750 mosquito nets to caregivers in Sinazongwe.
- $174,000 to provide a school for the Dalit people of India.

2010

- $25,000 to build and supply a thousand backpacks to children in Twachiyanda, Zambia.

- $3,500 to Hands & Feet Project for earth-quake relief in Haiti.
- $114,000 to build eight teacher houses at the Jonathan Sim School in Twachiyanda.

Austin has a book out whose title reiterates the point I hope you will grasp in this chapter: *Take Your Best Shot: Do Something Bigger Than Yourself.* One of the Bible verses Austin reflects upon as he speaks about Hoops of Hope is 1 Timothy 4:12: "Let no one look down on your youthfulness, but rather in speech, conduct, love, faith and purity, show yourself an example of those who believe."

"I'm happy and I'm proud that kids are finally seeing that they can make a difference at a young age, that they don't have to wait to be an adult," Austin said. "At the same time, it's hard to be proud of what we've done when you go to Africa and see how much more there is to do."

Wow!

The faith of a child—a child who saw a video about orphans in Africa, and refused to let the memory of it die. A child who felt a burden and realized, with God's help, he could move mountains.

You may be a housewife with children in school. Do you have a passion for keeping them safe, for keeping drugs and violence out of the school hallways? Perhaps you should start a ladies prayer group with other mothers in your community?

Maybe you're a high school teacher who's been entrusted with a classroom full of students. How will you steward the hearts and minds of those kids who've been placed in your care?

Say you're a college student. You've been entrusted with an education. What will you do with that knowledge and experience? How will you invest it for the good of others?

Listen to how the servants who were given five talents and two talents responded. "*Immediately* the one who had received the five talents went and traded with them, and gained five more talents. In the same manner the one who had received the two talents gained two more" (Matt. 25:16, 17, emphasis mine).

Now listen to the story of John Coors, chairman, president, and CEO of CoorsTek Inc. John and his wife

Sharna are the parents of ten children, six of whom are adopted. In 2001, John wanted to find out more about his African child's roots, so he flew to Nairobi, Kenya.

During the flight, on a jet in the pitch-black sky above sub-Saharan Africa, John woke up and stared out at the Sahara Desert. Looking down, he knew millions of people lived below, but there were no lights. It was at that moment that John says he felt God inviting him to do something about it.

A plan came to mind to bring people out of darkness using modern energy—the Circle of Light. Launched in Kenya in 2003, Circle of Light provided portable propane cook stoves, low-voltage lighting kits, and energy distribution services to rural communities. The impact on families and communities was visible. The results were vividly seen in the mending of marriages, the growing level of children's educations (because they could now see to read past dark!), and a greater expression of love and harmony in the home.

Unfortunately, after reaching nearly 12,000 families in twenty-three Kenyan and Mozambican communities, the Circle of Light collapsed in 2008, a victim of local greed, tribal clashes, and a non-profit business model. But John did not allow the dream to die and a restart, for-profit called Axxess Energy was launched in 2010. "The need has only grown," John said, "with over thirty million still cooking with wood in Kenya alone." The for-profit platform will allow for an investment by outsiders into improving the lives of millions in Africa in a way that will make the change permanent.

Has God made your heart beat to a special drum, like John Coors? What abilities has he given you? What fire burns in your belly? What are you "naturally" good at? What touches your heart emotionally and makes it beat in unison with God's?

Discussion Questions

1) Don't say what they are yet, but do you believe God has given you some truly unique talents and abilities?

2) According to the parable of the talents, what are you supposed to do with those talents and abilities?

3) What talent—be it treasure or ability or passion or skill—has God entrusted to you today? What passion has he woven into your heart, and only your heart?

4) Think about Sean Lambert's mission trip to Mexico and how his daughter asked him if they were going to build more houses. Has God ever hit you with a similar, almost overwhelming challenge? Explain and discuss.

5) Consider Austin Gutwein's story and 1 Timothy 4:12, then discuss whether age, circumstances, or "degree of difficulty" should stop you from investing the unique talents and abilities God has given you.

6) The ministry God has put in your lap today may not seem "glorious." Is that difficult for you? Discuss.

4

WHAT HAS HE ENTRUSTED TO YOU?

Use it or lose it

People of talent resemble a musical instrument
more closely than they do a musician. Without
outside help, they produce not a single sound,
but given even the slightest touch, and a
magnificent tune emanates from them.

— Franz Grillparzer

"How does the parable of the talents apply to me?" you might ask. "What is God trying to say?"

Those are the questions that nagged at me after hearing my good friend and mentor, Bruce Wilkinson, address a large group of pastors. He had just asked them, "If the Lord returned today and asked for an account of the 'talent' he had entrusted into your life, what could you tell God that you had brought back in exchange for the talent he'd given you?"

Although I was confused about what God was trying to say to me, it was clear as a bell that he had given those pastors their congregations. Those men were responsible for increasing the Kingdom of God, in numbers and impact. It was a no-brainer figuring out what someone else's ROT (return on talent) should be! If a pastor started with fifty people and grew his church to a hundred, *that* was good ROT. Or, if that congregation caught a glimpse of how God could use that team of fifty to reach hundreds if not thousands of people, that would be staggering!

But what about me? What was my talent? What possessions had God given me in which to invest?

Knowledge?

Experience?

People?

Talent?

Was I being responsible with his investment?

Was it growing or shrinking?

After letting Bruce's message percolate in my mind, I began to study the parable of the talents to see how I could and should be applying it in my life. At the time, I worked at Walk Thru the Bible (WTB), a non-profit Christian organization that produced Bible teaching, training, seminars, and publications on an international scale. As Director of Development, my job was to cultivate relationships with donors who periodically gave of their financial resources to WTB.

Suddenly, I was plagued with some soul-piercing questions. How was I treating the donors with whom I'd developed relationships. And what about my co-workers? Had I been a good and true friend to all? Did I genuinely care about them as individuals? Was I honest and forthright with them? Was my only goal to raise money or to love and care for the people God had brought into my life?

Sheesh.

They were heavy questions.

As I began to answer them with honesty and a desire to please God through my actions, beautiful things started to happen, things that line up perfectly with the parable of the talents.

The number of relationships I found myself cultivating grew. Soon I was playing the part of friend and counselor as I got into other peoples' lives and truly cared. Over the next five years, our pool of donors and ambassadors at WTB grew from several dozen to more than 1,400. Meanwhile, our contribution revenue climbed from $2 million a year to $9.3 million. Our sustained growth was running at an unprecedented thirty to thirty-five percent.

And guess what?

Personally, I was enjoying incomparable affirmation from the board and leadership at WTB, from donor families, peers, and staff. In a way, I felt like I was hearing, "Well done, good and faithful servant."

Along with our growth as an organization, my role and responsibilities increased. I managed special projects. My borders were bulging. I felt as if God was saying, "You were faithful with a few things, I will put you in charge of many things."

And I was so fulfilled! I was happy and motivated, excited and enthusiastic. At the time, I was operating in the sweet spot of my talent. The team at WTB felt God smiling as he said, "Enter into my joy!"

Friends and colleagues were noticing the work I was doing and began to challenge me. One in particular encouraged me to share my knowledge and experience with other organizations so they could perhaps realize the same type of growth, ultimately expanding the Kingdom of God.

With approval from the leadership at WTB, I began investing small segments of time with Moody Bible Institute, teaching them how to open their doors to new donors, ambassadors, and supporters. We designed a similar strategy at Moody as we had at WTB. Implementing the first phase, we showcased the work of Moody to see if donors would respond, and boy did they! Eventually, Moody would attribute $40 million in new revenue and hundreds of new partnerships to the work we did together.

You talk about "pure joy" and a spiritual high!

Whew, I was cruising!

But wait a second.

You know as well as I do that life is not always a smooth sail; our boats get rocked at times.

Mine was about to.

Why?

*In order to invest **all** the talents God had given me, it was going to require blind faith. Faith to step out and go where I'd never ventured before.*

Because, God had *more* for me. And he had more for those whose lives and ministries I could touch with the talents he'd given me.

Little did I realize at the time, but in order to invest *all* the talents God had given me, it was going to require blind faith. Faith to step out and go where I'd never ventured before. Faith to say, "Okay, Lord, I feel you leading me to take this giant leap—and I'm trusting you to help me fly!"

That's the kind of faith I needed after having a heart-to-heart with my friend Chris Crane, who at the time was the CEO of the largest Christian microfinance company in the world. "Bob, what would be a better use of your gifts?" he challenged. "Investing all of them in one organization, or investing them in more than one organization?"

As we continued to talk, Chris forced me to consider my real God-given talent. To him, it was a "no-brainer" that I was designed to team up with several organizations to develop powerful growth strategies. "Bob, I wonder if God called you to one specific organization," he probed, "or equipped you with specific gifts that could help many organizations?"

That's when the lights came on. Suddenly, I knew God wanted me to leverage the one or two talents he'd given me and multiply them exponentially to achieve an even more significant ROT! Was it a risk? Yes! I had four children, a daughter about to start college, and no money in the bank.

But I had no choice. I couldn't imagine facing God at the finish line and having to confess, "Master, I was afraid to take the risk and leverage the talents you gave me. So, I played it safe and stayed within the comfort zone of that one organization. I'm sorry, Lord. The pay was good, the benefits were solid, I was in a comfortable routine . . . ."

Know what the parable of the talents says about the servant who was given one talent, was afraid, and chose not to invest it? "But his master answered and said to him, 'You wicked, lazy slave, you knew that I reap where I did not sow, and gather where I scattered no seed. Then you ought to have put my money in the bank, and on my arrival I would have received my money back with interest. Therefore take away the talent from him, and give it to the one who has the ten talents" (Matt. 25:26-28).

So, you see, I *had to* venture out into the unknown.

That's when The Westfall Group was born (westfallgroup.net).

At the time, my "dream" was to help three to five organizations raise a total of $15 million.

Did God come through?

The Westfall Group began with two clients. After much hard work, and faith that our obedience would pay dividends, each of those clients enjoyed tremendous growth in revenue. Then there were three, four, five clients, all within that first year; each reaping astounding returns.

In the past eight years, we have become a leading provider of major gift fund development strategies. We've been fortunate enough to work with more than forty-five clients—including Fellowship of

Christian Athletes, Turning Point with David Jeremiah, Appalachia Service Project, Open Doors, Luis Palau, Mission to the World, Opportunity International, and many more—and watched more than $230 million flow into these organizations so they can pursue their dreams for ministry.

A man-sized dream had lived itself out in a God-sized reality.

Now *that's* ROT.

Speaking of that friend of mine, Chris Crane, you'll be floored by his story, the abilities God gave him, and the extraordinary ways God has used him. Chris was an MBA graduate of the Harvard Business School and a *for*-profit entrepreneur. Early in his career, he bought a publishing company that had lost money for five years in a row and, like magic, turned it into an electronic database publisher that went public in 1999.

He sold the company in 2000, and shortly there-after, was contacted by Opportunity International (opportunity.org), an organization that provides microfinance loans, savings, insurance, and training to hundreds of thousands of people working their way out of poverty in the developing world. Opportunity

International wanted Chris to become their president and CEO.

"Initially, I was reluctant, because I was a for-profit entrepreneur and wondered if I would be effective as a ministry CEO," Chris said. "However, the Lord made His many commands to serve the poor start jumping off the page during my daily Scripture readings. I felt he was calling me and I responded. I found the work very fulfilling."

Fulfilling *and* effective. Today, Opportunity International has provided its services to more than five million people in developing countries. It is the largest Christian microfinance organization in the world with a staff of 10,600 working in thirty-two countries. During Chris's tenure, Opportunity grew from 375,000 clients to 1.5 million, with revenue from private donors growing from $8 million to $51 million, a compound annual rate of thirty percent.

God knows what he is doing, my friend. He puts specific skills and abilities in specific people. By the way, after seven years at Opportunity International, Chris followed God's lead again and became the CEO of Edify, Inc. (www.edify.org), a humanitarian organization that makes small business loans to Christian schools educating impoverished children in Africa and Latin America. These sustainable schools charge tuition of just $5 to $10 per month and repay their loans, which are then loaned to other schools. Edify hopes to finance schools educating one million children over the next five years.

What an impact from just one man!

What about you? Is your joy increasing each day? Are you tapping into your distinct talents? In your case, is God able to say, "You were faithful with a few things, I will put you in charge of many things?"

Discussion Questions

1) How does the parable of the talents apply to you? At this point in the book, what is God trying to show you?

2) If the Lord returned today and asked for an account of the "talents" he had entrusted into your life, what could you tell him? What is your "return on investment," or, in this case, "return on talent"?

3) How are you treating the "ministry" that is yours today—even if it isn't glamorous? Are you cultivating it? Developing relationships? Caring about others more than yourself? Giving it the energy and attention it requires and deserves?

4) Do you sense God saying, "Well done, good and faithful servant?" Or could he possibly be whispering, "In need of improvement?"

5) Sometimes, in order to invest all the talents God has given you, it requires blind faith. Is that true in your case? Discuss.

6) Have you ever imagined meeting God at the finish line and having to confess, "Master, I was afraid to take the risk and leverage the talents you gave me. I played it safe and stayed within my comfort zone. I kept my status quo job—the benefits were too good to pass up"? Discuss.

5

TAKE CHANCES, GET MESSY

God LOVES radical faith in action

Hide not your talents, they for use were made.
What's a sundial in the shade?

— Benjamin Franklin

Larry Page, founder of the wildly popular Internet search engine, Google, said this: "We were so afraid that Google might fail that we contemplated not starting the company."[1]

The fact is, when we are *led* to do something, when we feel God *urging us on* to do that one thing only we have the creativity, compassion, desire, or talent to do, then all of the fears of failure must be thrown aside.

All of the naysayers must be ignored.

All of the impossible odds must not dishearten us.

And all of the dependence upon ourselves must be relinquished.

Let me ask you a question. Do you believe—really believe—the statement from the Bible that says: "Unless the Lord builds the house, they labor in vain who build it; unless the Lord guards the city, the watchman keeps awake in vain" (Ps. 127:1)?

Do you believe that he is the mighty one who trains your hands for battle, so that your arms can bend a bow of bronze (2 Sam. 22:35)?

It is not up to you and me to worry about results. It is up to you and me to figure out what God wants us to do—and to do it. If he is with you in the dream he has placed in your heart, nothing can stop it from unfolding the way he wants it to, no matter how impossible it may seem.

It is not up to you and me to worry about results.
It is up to you and me to figure out what
God wants us to do—and to do it.

Over thirty years ago, Don Schoendorfer watched a disabled Moroccan woman drag herself across a dirt road in a foreign land. The mental image of her anguish and loss of dignity haunted him for years, until 1999 when Don gave in to God's prompting to do something about it.

You see, Don not only had recurring thoughts about the handicapped Moroccan woman and a desire to help the millions of people who can't walk, he also had a PhD in mechanical engineering. So, he created a simple, rugged, inexpensive wheelchair made of a plastic lawn chair, a steel frame, and a pair of bicycle tires.

When Don realized such wheelchairs could be built and shipped for under $60 each, Free Wheelchair Mission was born (www.freewheelchairmission.org). Since then, the ministry has distributed over 550,000 wheelchairs to people with disabilities in seventy-eight countries, including South America, Africa, Latin America and the Caribbean, Eastern Europe, the Middle East, Asia, and the Pacific.

Did you get that?

Over 550,000 free wheelchairs.

Do you see it?

"You were faithful with a few things, I will put you in charge of many things."

A volunteer for Free Wheelchair Mission, Ines Franklin, says, "When one of our recipients gets seated in that chair for the first time, it's magical."

Another volunteer says, "When you lift somebody off the ground, it by far overshadows any other experience."

Do the words, "Enter into the joy of your master," come to mind?

I can just see the Lord smiling when Don and his team seat someone in one of those wheelchairs who's been crawling his entire life, and say, "This wheelchair is for you. We want you to feel like you are resting in God's hands when you sit in it."

I don't know about you, but to me, *that* is ministry.

To me, *that* is true religion.

It's a breath of fresh air.

And it's life being lived to the fullest.

It's life abundant, which is what Christ calls us to.

It's pure joy!

And get this. The goal of Free Wheelchair Mission is to provide *twenty million* wheelchairs to those in

Figuring out what God wants can be the most difficult part of our life's journey. But when we finally do figure out what he is leading us to do—we must step out in faith knowing that he will pave the way.

need. "These people are on the ground now, waiting," says Don. "They're waiting for us to provide a wheelchair. We don't want to take a hundred years to solve this problem. There's no reason why we can't begin to solve it now."

Who gave Don his ability?

Who allowed him to see that Moroccan woman?

Who put the desire in his heart to do something?

God did.

And Don was obedient.

He didn't get caught up worrying that he was only one man with a strange and radical idea in his head. He moved forward, one step at a time.

There was grunt work involved. It wasn't easy. There was no "promise" his idea would succeed. But with God driving the plan, Don could not fail. And neither could Free Wheelchair Mission.

Many times, figuring out what God wants can be the most difficult part of our life's journey. But when we finally do figure out what he is leading us to do— no matter how odd or unlikely or impossible it may seem—we must step out in faith knowing that he will pave the way.

This reminds me of the intriguing story of a man I know named Bernie May. Bernie grew up in a Christian home, reading and memorizing the Bible, and recalls becoming a Christian at the age of eleven. However, after high school, when he ventured off to college, church became irrelevant to him. It wasn't that he stopped believing in God; instead, he became busy pursuing his studies and planning to provide for the young lady of his dreams, Nancy, whom he married during his senior year of college.

Bernie had a promising career lined up and so did Nancy. During their first year of marriage they never attended church, thinking that they were way too busy for it. But their life's agenda was shaping up beautifully. They were each on track with their careers, their marriage was sound, they were building a life together—on their way to fulfilling "the American dream."

Somewhere along the line early on in their marriage, however, Bernie and Nancy picked up their Bibles. As many of us know, that can be a life-changing endeavor. Suddenly, reading the Bible again as an adult, God's truth revived itself in Bernie's mind and he was struck by the clarity and power of the words. The sayings of Jesus were radical and pierced Bernie like a heavenly surgeon performing an intricate operation on his very heart. What kind of life was Jesus calling Bernie to? Soon, while examining himself in the mirror of God's Word, he was questioning whether or not he was even a Christian! Bernie even recalls thinking this precise thought: "I either need to stop calling myself a Christian, or my life needs to change."

Just like that, Bernie realized God had an agenda for his life—and it was completely different than his own agenda, than Nancy's, or than the "American dream." He realized God had some sort of mysterious, overarching plan, and he began thinking deeply about what his role was supposed to be? What was the meaning of life? Why was he here? What was his purpose?

While driving in his car one day during that period, Bernie had what he calls a visitation from the Holy Spirit. He was overwhelmed. The awesomeness of God's presence caused Bernie to surrender his life to Jesus and he chose to live by faith in the Son of God. On the spot, Bernie gave up his own agenda and vowed to do what God wanted him to do. Suddenly, Bernie felt significance and knew he would never be the same.

Although Bernie did not know what God had in store for him, he knew one thing: he needed to get home and tell Nancy what had happened. Would she think he was crazy? That he'd gone off the deep end?

When Bernie walked in the door, anxious to share with Nancy what had happened, she trumped him. "Something happened to me while you were gone," she said. "I surrendered my life to Christ!"

Amazing?

To say the least.

God knows what he's doing.

Look at the team he put together in Bernie and Nancy.

What happened next?

The first thing they agreed to do was go to church because, after all, that was what Christians did, right? But Bernie was skeptical. He'd pulled away from the church years earlier. Could he go back? The next week, he and Nancy actually drove to the church where Bernie had grown up.

How good is God's timing?

That Sunday there was a special speaker at the church—a young female missionary from Wycliffe Bible Translators. Her story was absolutely compelling. She spoke of the work Wycliffe was doing, translating the scriptures so that every language and people group would have access to the Bible.

Bernie and Nancy felt drawn to Wycliffe's vision and mission, and to what this young lady was doing with her life. It was a greater agenda; God's agenda. Although Bernie and Nancy were intrigued by the young woman's presentation, the problem was that they were not missionaries and they certainly were not linguists.

But then it happened. God's timing. His plan. Revealed.

Somewhere during the young lady's presentation, she mentioned that two of Wycliffe's greatest needs were for pilots and secretaries. It completely knocked Bernie and Nancy for a loop. Why? Bernie had obtained his pilot's license. He had done it out of sheer interest, as a hobby, never thinking he would use the license for anything other than periodic pleasure journeys. To top that, Nancy was a professional secretary.

Bernie whispered that perhaps this was it, God's plan for their lives.

Nancy hesitated. "We're not the missionary type."

Bernie hesitated, too. "Maybe they won't notice!"

Two weeks later, they found themselves stepping out in faith, taking off for South America with Wycliffe, Bernie as a bush pilot and Nancy as a secretary. That was in 1954. And what a journey it's been since then.

Bernie served as a pilot for Wycliffe in Peru and Ecuador for sixteen years. His business background and drive for innovation gained broad attention, and he later served as president of JAARS, a Wycliffe-affiliated technical organization, for five years. After that, he became president of Wycliffe USA for twelve years. In 1982, Bernie helped launch the Bibleless Peoples Prayer Project, Wycliffe's intercessory prayer effort.

By the late 1980s, Wycliffe realized it would take 150 years at its current pace of translation to reach every people group, so they asked Bernie to lead an initiative to build a model that would accelerate the pace by involving more national leadership. So, in 1993, Bernie founded The Seed Company. It was a Wycliffe initiative to connect investors with national-led translation projects.

Since its founding, The Seed Company has translated the Bible into 700 languages and is currently working in more than 400 languages with the potential to impact over 800 million people in those language communities.

Bernie's work took him to sixty countries where he had the opportunity to see God at work "in all the world." At almost eighty years of age, Bernie continues to work with both Wycliffe and The Seed Company in a consulting and advisory role. "You can retire from your job, but you can't retire from your calling," he said. "Making the Bible available to all people in their own language is what God has given me to do with my life. I recently spent time with a minority language group in China for whom I pray each day. And I fund six young

Chinese women who are translating the Bible into their mother tongue!"

The life Bernie has lived is nothing he would have planned for himself and, in fact, has proven to be far beyond what he could have ever thought or imagined. He has taken a journey into the mystery of God's great story. He has learned what it means to live by faith.

So now, back to you.

What abilities or talents has God given you?

Who has he allowed you to see? What has he permitted you to experience?

What passion has he put on your heart?

What door has he opened?

And finally . . . what are you waiting for?

Discussion Questions

1) Often there is fear in pursuing God's dreams for you. Do you believe the statement from the Bible that says: "Unless the Lord builds the house, they labor in vain who build it; unless the Lord guards the city, the watchman keeps awake in vain" (Ps. 127:1)? Do you believe that he is the Mighty One who trains your hands for battle, so that your arms can bend a bow of bronze (2 Sam. 22: 35)? Discuss.

2) Discuss this statement: "It is not up to you and me to worry about results. It is up to you and me to figure out what God wants us to do—and do it."

3) Review the story of Don Schoendorfer. Visit the Free Wheelchair Mission website: www.freewheelchairmission.org. How does Don's story compare with yours? What does his story make you want to do?

4) Often, in doing what God wants us to do, there is grunt work involved, it isn't easy, and there are no promises that it will succeed. If this is true of your circumstances, how does this make you feel? How can you overcome that feeling of the tasks or work you are doing being insignificant??

5) How are you unique? What has God allowed you to see? Whom has he allowed you to meet? What has he permitted you to experience? What door has he opened? What are you waiting for?

---

1.   *Fortune Magazine*, May 12, 2008

6

YOU ARE ARMED
AND DANGEROUS

Invest what you've been given
and watch the joy fall like rain

*Work while you have light. You are responsible
for the talent that has been entrusted to you.*

— Henri Frederick Amiel

L et me make an essential point here: God has *already
given you* the talent, ability, skill, money, or passion
you need to fulfill his plan, to be entrusted with more,
and to walk in pure joy. That's one of the key truths of
the parable of the talents that many people miss.

Remember?

The master went on a journey. But before he left,
he called his servants in and "entrusted his possessions
to them" (Matt. 25:14b). He passed out five talents to

one, two to another, and one to a third, "each according to his own ability," and then he went on his way.

What I'm trying to show you is that you *already have* everything you need! The skill is within you. The dream is deep inside you. The plan is in place. The passion is there. The ability is woven into your DNA by the creator himself.

Have you examined your life?

The people within your circles?

The possibilities within your realm?

That young man I visited in Texas had overlooked his two co-workers and the two couples in his Sunday school class. They were right under his nose!

Will you be faithful in the little things?

Examine your life today.

Don't make the mistake of saying, "Someday, when I have this, I'll do that," or, "When I have more time, I'll pursue that dream," or, "When I have more money, I'll give to this or that organization."

If Don Schoendorfer had done that, there would be 550,000 more disabled people in the world today without wheelchairs. If Sean Lambert had done that, there would be thousands more people without homes. If John

Coors had done that, there would be nearly 12,000 more families without lighting and cooking kits in Africa.

And if Gary Skinner had done that, there would be 2,000 more orphans in Uganda. But Gary chose not to ignore God's calling.

Oh, he tried all right.

Gary and his wife Marilyn were missionaries in Africa and had founded a church in Kampala, Uganda, called Watoto Church. They labored and the church grew from next to nothing to 18,000 members.

But then God prompted Gary to reach out to the scores of widows and orphans in the area.

As Gary tells it, "I told God, 'Lord, I came here to run this church.'"

But God told him, "You need to reach out to the widows and orphans."

"No, God," Gary responded. "I'm here to run this big church. You know that."

"No," God said. "You're here to reach out to the widows and orphans of this community."

"But I don't want to deal with snotty-nosed, big-bellied, fly-in-the-eye children!"

"But that's what I've built you to do."

And so Watoto Child Care Ministries was born (watoto.com).

Since its inception, the ministry has rescued more than 2,000 orphans from lives of despair. The loving people from Watoto build children's villages in Africa, including anywhere from thirty-five to 150 homes. They place the children in a home with one house-mother—usually a widow—and eight children. That becomes their 'forever family.' Within the villages, they build schools, medical clinics, community centers/churches, and create self-sustainability through farming. For the children, unconditional love and spiritual discipleship abound. The physical needs of the children are met and they are equipped with moral values and life skills that will enable them to live lives of significance and become leaders and agents of change in Uganda. But Gary and Marilyn's ministry doesn't stop in Africa. Amazingly, thirty-seven such villages have been built around the world!

Visiting an orphanage where her mom worked in China, my wife, Kim, was struck by the way the parentless little ones reached out to her for human contact. "It was one of the worst days of my life," Kim recalls.

"Seeing those poor kids, my heart was gripped. I was a wreck; in tears. Couldn't stop thinking about their need for the love of a mom and dad, and how desperate they were for human affection."

That vivid memory never left Kim and guess what?

She went on to manage the U.S. office for Watoto Child Care Ministries.

The ministry began with two orphans. They used the money that had been donated wisely and faithfully, people gave more, and soon they had placed twenty orphans.

Then a hundred.

Then a thousand.

Their goal is to help 10,000 orphans find Christian homes. And out of those homes will come that continent's future leaders.

Do you see how Gary and Marilyn took the talents and abilities God gave them and faithfully invested them in others? The return has been unfathomable—and priceless.

What I want to declare to you today is, take the seed that God planted in you and water it, nurture it—don't let anything keep it from sprouting!

Ever since my wife Kim's visit to that orphanage in China, and throughout her work with Watoto, she realized that one of the talents God knit in her heart was a passion and devotion for children at risk. It is that inbred love that led her to become the U.S. Director for a ministry called Grain of Wheat International, founded by a prosperous Swiss businessman named Jean Andre—who proved to be armed and dangerous, and who followed his life's calling.

Traveling through Germany in 1948, Jean found himself utterly devastated by the condition of the helpless victims of World War II. His heart felt crushed as he witnessed countless orphans clinging to life in the ruins of shattered city after shattered city.

With his own money, Jean rented—and later purchased—two large homes where war-orphaned children would have an opportunity to start their lives again. With a heartfelt mission to provide more than just shelter and food, Jean made sure the children were educated in their mother tongue, taught of God's love, and returned to their homelands far better equipped to become everything God had called them to be. Thus began the work of "Grain de Blé," Grain of Wheat International.

Today, more than sixty years after Jean first poured out his heart to war orphans, his ministry continues to extend hope to children from all backgrounds, in all situations—and to impart the love of the Heavenly Father to each one. In fact, Jean's talents have been multiplied by God—exponentially! For the first twenty years his ministry helped about six hundred children per year, each child staying for about three months. From 1970 to 1990, shorter camps were offered, a school was added, and about one thousand children were helped each year—in eight countries.

From 1990 to 2000, an average of 20,000 children a year were helped by Grain of Wheat International, which had reached into eighteen countries. And between 2000 and 2010, Jean's ministry was helping 200,000 children per year, for a total of two million children helped—in thirty-two countries!

You cannot out-give God.

Test him.

Surrender your life and work to him.

> *You were designed for a purpose! When you discover what that purpose is and begin walking in it, pure joy always comes next.*

Will he not throw open the floodgates of heaven and pour out so much blessing that there won't be room enough to store it?

It's all about stewarding what God has given you.

Are you stewarding your talents faithfully?

Wisely?

Diligently?

The thing to remember is, your best *is* good enough. You were designed for a purpose! When you discover what that purpose is and begin walking in it, pure joy always comes next.

Question: What inspired the people at Watoto Child Care Ministries to want to help 10,000 orphans in Uganda?

Answer: The joy they experienced from being a conduit to help two desperately poor children transition to a wonderful life!

Question: What caused Jean Andre's ministry to grow and grow and grow, so more orphan's could be loved and nurtured and prepared for the future?

Answer: One man, being obedient to the small voice he heard, telling him to rent those first two houses and help a handful of orphans.

I want to tell you about another man who was destined to be a mechanical engineer, but tragedy struck his life—and he turned out to be a life-saver. His name is Parker H. "Pete" Petit, and the home medical monitor he invented saved my daughter Jessica's life!

It was the summer of 1970. Up to that point, everything was going "as planned." Pete had earned his bachelor's and master's degrees in mechanical engineering from the Georgia Institute of Technology, and had a promising job as a project manager at Lockheed in Marietta, Georgia. Suddenly, however, Pete's infant son Brett died in his crib. Overnight, Pete and his wife joined the thousands of parents whose children had lost their lives in crib deaths to Sudden Infant Death Syndrome (SIDS).

As Pete and his wife mourned and tried to keep going, questions plagued Pete about why this had happened, how, and if it could have been prevented? He soon learned that deaths similar to Brett's were being prevented, but only in hospitals where expensive monitoring units were available to prevent death in newborns.

Pete had an idea. What if someone were to create and develop a smaller, portable monitoring unit that people could rent and have in their homes when their children were at risk for SIDS? And what if that someone was Pete?

From that moment on, the "naïve" Pete poured everything he had into the new life-saving creation. He resigned from his job at Lockheed in early 1971 and he took night classes to earn his M.B.A. at Georgia State University, where he learned more about business and finance. While he was taking classes, he raised funding and founded a company that would later become Healthdyne, Inc., manufacturer of high technology healthcare devices, provider of healthcare information systems, technology, healthcare services, and disease management.

Pete had a plan for his life, but the death of his son re-directed it. He took his grief and turned it into passion for saving lives by creating an affordable, take-home respiratory and heart monitor that monitors over 10,000 infants a year. Over all, the monitor has saved tens of thousands of infants, including my now twenty-year-old daughter, Jessica, who was monitored as an infant when her life was threatened by SIDS.

But Pete didn't stop there—far from it. In order to increase shareholder value, Healthdyne was split into three publicly traded companies whose annual revenues grew in excess of $1 billion in 1996. Pete has served on the board of directors and board of trustees for major corporations and organizations, including Atlantic Southeast Airlines, Intelligent Systems, and the National Health Museum. He has donated millions of dollars to a variety of worthy philanthropy projects.

Just like Pete and Gary and Don, and just like the headline at the beginning of this chapter—*you* are armed and dangerous! Isn't it time *you* followed *your calling?*

I urge you—plumb the depths of the parable of the talents.

Take a good, hard look at the context of your life— where you've been, what's happened to you, where

> *Nothing happens by chance. You are where you are*
> *and the way you are for a reason, for God's reason.*

you're going. Nothing happens by chance. You are where you are and the way you are for a reason, for God's reason.

The master says that when you invest the talents he's given you, when you are faithful to bear fruit from the little he's given you, he will give you more. And you will enter into his joy.

People around the world are searching for joy.

Where is it?

How can we find it?

Here's the answer. Plain and simple. Straight from God: invest what I've given you. Take a chance. Put it to work. Trust me. Make it multiply. Then I'll give you more. And you'll be happier and more content than you ever fathomed.

Don't believe it?

Think of investing your talents the way the Old Testament describes giving your tithe. "'Test me now in this,' says the Lord of hosts, 'if I will not open for you the windows of heaven, and pour out for you a blessing until it overflows'" (Mal. 3:10b).

We've all heard it said, "You can't out-give God."

He's made me a believer.

My joy is worth more than all the money in a zillion banks.

What about you?

Are you ready to take a good, hard look at yourself and determine what talents God has knit together within you?

Discussion Questions

1) Do you believe this statement: God has already given you the talent, ability, skill, or passion you need to fulfill his plan, to be entrusted with more, and to walk in pure joy? Discuss.

2) Have you ever fallen into the trap of saying, "Someday, when I have this, I'll do that," or, "When I have more time, I'll pursue that dream," or, "When I have more money, I'll give to this or that organization?" Discuss.

3) Gary Skinner recalled, "I told God, 'Lord, I came here to run this church.'" But God told him, "You need to reach out to the widows and orphans." Has God ever revealed a plan involving you that you simply did not like and that was not your plan? Explain and discuss.

4) What really grips your heart and pulls at your emotions? For my wife Kim it was seeing an orphanage full of desperate children in China. For Jean Andre it was witnessing the helpless victims devastated by World War II in Germany. What really makes your heart pound with passion? Could that be your calling? Discuss.

5) Discuss the following: You cannot out-give God. Test him. Surrender your life and work to him. Will he not throw open the floodgates of heaven and pour out so much blessing that there won't be room enough to store it?

6) For Pete Petit, a miracle was born out of a tragedy. Could this be true in your case? Explain and discuss.

7

MAKE A
POSITIVE I.D.

Isn't it time you followed your calling?

Use what talents you possess;
the woods would be very silent
if no birds sang there except those that sang best.

— Attributed to both William Blake and Henry Van Dyke

What are your "talents"? What were you designed to do before the earth started turning?

Something beckons you, calls your name, burns within.

It matters not if you're a doctor or teacher, mother or father, executive or electrician, student or senior, pastor or painter, decorator or doorman, spouse or single, entrepreneur or assembly line worker.

We are each "His workmanship, created in Christ Jesus for good works, which God prepared beforehand, that we should walk in them" (Eph. 2:10).

What God values most is the return we bring on the investment he's left with us.

If you're a busy individual, like most of us, let me encourage you to take a moment to stop everything else you might be doing right now, get alone, get quiet, and answer a few potentially life-changing questions.

But before you do that, I invite you to ask God for his wisdom and insight as you answer these questions. Ask him what his expectations are of you. Ask him to help you understand the talents he has invested into your life. And ask him to help you understand how to double those talents and bring him magnificent ROT.

> *For if you cry for discernment, lift your voice for understanding;*
>
> *If you seek her as silver, and search for her as for hidden treasures;*
>
> *Then you will discern the fear of the Lord, and discover the knowledge of God.*

For the Lord gives wisdom; from his mouth come knowledge and understanding. (Prov. 2:3-6).

I firmly believe God has implanted our passions and desires within us to lead us to our talents! To that end, ask yourself the following questions (and jot down your answers):

- What are you extremely good at?

- What comes naturally for you?

- What are you interested in?

- What are you passionate about and
  drawn to?

  _____

  _____

  _____

- Of all the things you do, what brings you
  the greatest joy?

  _____

  _____

  _____

- What ministries seem to really "fit"
  your passion?

  _____

  _____

  _____

- What is it you do that, when you are
  finished, you find yourself saying, "Holy
  Toledo, I can't wait to do that again!"

  _____

  _____

_____

_____

- What has been your most life-altering experience?

_____

_____

_____

- In what area do you have the greatest impact on other people?

_____

_____

_____

Because your passions and "talents" may not always line up with the career or calling in which you currently find yourself, the key for you is going to be finding a way to merge your passions with your present-day realities.

A man I met recently has done that without missing a beat. His name is Hyatt Moore. Hyatt has devoted most of his life to seeing the Bible translated into hundreds of languages. He's led organizations I've mentioned earlier in the book—The Seed Company and

Wycliffe Bible Translators—and has had a tremendous impact in this field. Hyatt is passionate about reaching different people groups with the Bible.

So, what happens later in his life?

Hyatt begins to paint. He takes a serious interest in art. He studies the greats. He makes time to paint. And in just over a decade, he becomes an outstanding artist with a solid reputation in the art world (hyatt-moore.com).

What does he do next?

Combines his two passions.

Take a look at the painting he created on the next page.

I was in attendance, along with a group of other people when Hyatt painted this work. The whole time he painted, I thought, "What a creative investment of talent!"

When he was finished painting, Hyatt proceeded to cut the picture up into seventy-two pieces and each of us in attendance was given a face to take home with us. I was moved beyond words. Each time I look at the face I was given, I'm reminded of the experience and Hyatt's passion to reach all people groups with the Bible.

An "in-process" moment of the mural Hyatt Moore was painting during our three-day conference. On 6 ft. x 8 ft. canvas, when finished there were a total of seventy-two small "portraits" painted in. What nobody knew was that in the end Hyatt would cut up the canvas and give each participant a portrait, matted and ready for framing."

What remarkable ROT!

Does Hyatt's story spark any ideas about your own life and how you can invest the "talents" God has instilled in you? Write down the thoughts, ideas, and dreams God brings to mind.

_____

_____

_____

_____

As you ponder your own gifts, abilities, and "talents," consider the amazing story of how Dr. Scott Harrison put his to work to bless others. He was an orthopedic surgeon with a thriving practice in the United States and several young partners, when he was invited by another surgeon to travel to Malawi, Africa, to perform and teach spinal surgery.

Initially, Dr. Harrison determined he would make one trip and that would be the end of it. But performing intricate, interesting procedures that were curing children and adults with spinal deformities in a Third World country was much more rewarding than he ever imagined. Soon, Dr. Harrison found himself returning for several months at a time and even looking for an American company to join in order to continue the work.

Later, back in the U.S., he was asked to take over as the CEO of a large New York Stock Exchange company that was failing. Initially, he was uninterested. Although he was gifted in business, it didn't seem like something God would have him do. But as he and his wife Sally began praying, it became clear to Dr. Harrison that he was supposed to take the job; it was, indeed, one of the few times in his life he received a positively clear answer to prayer. It seemed strange at the time and it confused him, but he was obedient and left his practice of twenty years to enter the corporate world. In the years that followed, he helped turn the company around, sold it in a merger, and was once again free to pursue his passion.

It didn't take Dr. Harrison long to return to Africa to continue helping the less fortunate and searching for an agency with whom he could work—but he found none. Sally and Scott took that to mean that it was their job to make it happen. Using his in-depth business experience and his passion and knowledge as a surgeon, he and Sally set out to begin CURE International.

Talk about dreaming big. When Scott and Sally were planning CURE, they drew directly from Jesus' example in the scriptures when he sent out the twelve and later the seventy-two to minister, instructing them to do two things: heal the sick and preach the gospel. This was important to the Harrisons, because they knew that most of the agencies in the U.S. that existed to help cure diseases overseas had at most a five percent focus on the gospel, if any, and that those organizations were almost always more about the surgeon than about the patients.

On another trip back to Africa, this time to Kenya, Dr. Harrison met another missionary who, "by chance," had a similar passion. Together, they opened their first hospital. That was twelve years ago. Today, CURE International (Cure.org) has eleven hospitals open in ten countries. They have performed 84,000 surgeries, treated more than 1.3 million patients, and have helped bring hundreds of thousands into continuing relationships with Jesus Christ.

If that doesn't give you chills, I don't know what will! And Scott and Sally have held steadfast to their plan and unique vision for CURE, which is to bring physical and spiritual healing to children with disabilities in the developing world. As I write this, CURE is

> *God gives us the freedom to say "no" to his dynamic plans. He'll let us live easily and anonymously in service to him ... but it won't be his best.*

transforming the lives of children with hydrocephalus, cleft lip and palate, spine deformities, clubfoot, and other crippling orthopedic conditions. These children and their families often feel great shame and face rejection from their relatives and communities, but at CURE, they find acceptance and hope as hospital staff members express God's love for them.

Remarkably, Scott is convinced that if he had not followed God's lead to make the leap into the corporate world years earlier, using a gift he knew he had but was unsure of its purpose, he would still be working in his medical practice.

God gives us the freedom to say "no" to his dynamic plans. He'll let us live easily and anonymously in service to him . . . but it won't be his best. It won't be all we can be. It won't be ultimately fulfilling.

Scott could have said no to the CEO position and, in essence, buried his talents. He could have given up on his dream to serve others with his gifts in Africa.

You might be right where he was at that point.

You have an idea.

You feel a passion to do something.

But the mountain looks too large or impossible to scale. The giants look too big to defeat. You're thinking, "What can one man or woman do? What impact can one person have? What can I contribute?"

Scott took a higher path, one I'm sure makes the Lord break out in laughter.

Jesus even came right out and said that when we feed the hungry, give drink to the thirsty, welcome the stranger, clothe the naked, and visit the sick—we are actually doing those things for him (Matt. 25:35-46).

Our lives are short, folks.

What will we do with them to help others?

How will we invest what's been given to us?

Watch and pray—your answer will come.

And when it does, get ready, because the joy to follow will be like none you've ever experienced.

Discussion Questions

1) Read this verse: We are each "His workmanship, created in Christ Jesus for good works, which God prepared beforehand, that we should walk in them" (Eph. 2:10). Pray that God will reveal himself and his plans to you. Then, read and discuss any or all of the following questions and your answers from Chapter 7:

- What are you extremely good at?

- What comes naturally for you?

- What are you interested in?

- What are you passionate about and drawn to?

- Of all the things you do, what brings you the greatest joy?

- What ministries seem to really 'fit' your passion?

- What is it you do that, when you are finished, you find yourself saying, "Holy Toledo, I can't wait to do that again!"

- What has been your most life-altering experience?

- In what area do you have the greatest impact on other people?

8

BURIED TREASURE ISN'T ALWAYS GOOD

Pure joy requires an investment

The artist is nothing without the gift,
but the gift is nothing without work.

— Emile Zola

Whether you're a parent or not, you can imagine how it feels to invest endless hours and resources, physical and mental energy, into your children, trying to instill godly morals and values into their lives. Being the father of four, I can tell you, parenting is a tiring and often thankless job. Like Dr. James Dobson says, parenting definitely isn't for cowards!

But there is an incomparable, almost indescribable feeling that can result in the process of parenting. And that happens when your children are obedient. When, with the unquestioning faith only a child can exude, they remember what you've taught them and simply put it into practice.

Your little boy halts at the curb to watch for traffic when a ball is kicked into the street.

Your little girl hurries to help her brother when he falls from his bicycle.

Your son tells the truth in a heated situation.

Your teenage daughter says she's not going to that sleepover because many of the girls are gossips.

Your college graduate says he's going to work for a non-profit that helps high-risk, inner-city children.

Imagine the emotions you experience as the parent.

Pure joy.

Not the joy you experienced when you got your first puppy or that came with your first kiss.

But when you give yourself up for God's use and invest your talents for his purpose, then you find the true meaning of life—and abundant joy. It's what you were meant for.

Not a rollercoaster joy that lasts only as long as the good circumstances.

I'm talking about a joy that is so deep-seated, so grassroots, it rises up from the very core of your being and permeates your mind and soul.

It's a joy no one can steal and nothing can extinguish.

It's a joy that embodies you and was created specifically for you by the author and creator of your life.

The joy of which I speak is the very essence of a fulfilled life.

Jesus said, "Whoever finds his life will lose it, and whoever loses his life for my sake will find it" (Matt. 10:39 ESV).

The Bob Westfall translation of that says, when you live for yourself, you never find the true meaning of life; you never experience pure joy. But when you give yourself up for God's use and invest your talents for his purpose, then you find the true meaning of life—and abundant joy.

It's what you were meant for.

Our creator experiences that same joy when you and I invest that which he has entrusted to us in ways that produce fruit.

"His master said to him, 'Well done, good and faithful slave. You were faithful with a few things, I will put you in charge of many things; *enter into the joy of your master*'" (Matt. 25:23, emphasis mine).

I believe it is what we do with the "talents" God has given us that determines the destiny of joy in our lives. Likewise, it is what we *do not* do with those talents that can set our lives on a different course.

I would be remiss if I failed to mention how the parable of the talents ends.

> And the one also who had received the one talent came up and said, "Master, I knew you to be a hard man, reaping where you did not sow, and gathering where you scattered no seed. And I was afraid, and went away and hid your talent in the ground; see, you have what is yours."
>
> But his master answered and said to him, "You wicked, lazy slave, you knew that I reap where I did not sow, and gather where I scattered no seed. Then you ought to have put my money in the bank, and on my arrival I would

have received my money back with interest. Therefore take away the talent from him, and give it to the one who has the ten talents. For to everyone who has shall more be given, and he shall have an abundance; but from the one who does not have, even what he does have shall be taken away. And cast out the worthless slave into the outer darkness; in that place there shall be weeping and gnashing of teeth." (Matt. 25:24-30)

The thing that blows my mind about the parable of the talents is that I believe Jesus was speaking literally about himself when he said he was about to go on a long journey. It's a journey that has culminated with him seated on his throne. One day, he will return just as he describes in the parable of the talents and today he says to each of us, "When I return, I want to know how you spent your time, what you did with your talents, and what you did with my possessions that I entrusted into your hands?"

This excites me. At the same time, it sobers me to the core.

Examining the parable of the talents in context we see that it is one in a string of responses Jesus gave to a pertinent question asked by the disciples: "What is the sign of your coming, and of the end of the age?" Following that, Jesus used a number of parables to paint a picture of his journey, what we should be doing while he is away, and what to expect when he returns.

Here are a few of the highlights leading up to the parable of the talents:

> Who then is the faithful and wise servant, whom the master has put in charge of the servants in his household to give them their food at the proper time? It will be good for that servant whose master finds him doing so when he returns. Truly I tell you, he will put him in charge of all his possessions. But suppose that servant is wicked and says to himself, "My master is staying away a long time," and he then begins to beat his fellow servants and to eat and drink with drunkards. The master of that servant will come on a day when he does not expect him and at an hour he is not aware

of. He will cut him to pieces and assign him a place with the hypocrites, where there will be weeping and gnashing of teeth. (Matt. 24:45-51 NIV)

At that time the kingdom of heaven will be like ten virgins who took their lamps and went out to meet the bridegroom. Five of them were foolish and five were wise. The foolish ones took their lamps but did not take any oil with them. The wise ones, however, took oil in jars along with their lamps. The bridegroom was a long time in coming, and they all became drowsy and fell asleep. At midnight the cry rang out: "Here's the bridegroom! Come out to meet him!" Then all the virgins woke up and trimmed their lamps. The foolish ones said to the wise, "Give us some of your oil; our lamps are going out." "No," they replied, "there may not be enough for both us and you. Instead, go to those who sell oil and buy some for yourselves." But while they were on their way to buy the oil, the bridegroom arrived. The virgins who were ready went in with him to the wedding banquet. And the door was shut. Later the others also came. "Lord, Lord," they said, "open the door for us!" But he replied, "Truly I tell you, I don't know you." Therefore keep watch, because you do not know the day or the hour. (Matt. 25:1-13 NIV)

As I study these verses I realize there is an almost tangible, palpable urgency in Christ's voice. He is urging us to be about his business during our brief time here on earth.

We don't see God now, but do we believe his Word? Is Jesus coming back? Is he serious about what he expects us to be doing while he is away? Is he going to reward us when he gets here, or possibly punish us?

The true but not politically correct answer is, Yes! The Lord of judgment is coming back. And when Christ returns he will settle accounts.

"Look, I am coming soon! My reward is with me, and I will give to each person according to what they have done" (Rev. 22:12 NIV).

Notice that the first thing on Christ's mind when he speaks of his return is rewarding those who have done well, used their time wisely, and invested the talents he's distributed. The scriptures indicate that he can't wait to get here to pay us back for our diligent work on his behalf.

Picture yourself about to go on a long journey. You are going to be gone so long it simply doesn't make sense to keep your most prized possessions stored up in a rental facility. So you go to three investors and make them a proposal. "Will you manage these possessions for me while I am away?" You give one person $50,000, another $20,000, and another $10,000.

You are gone for a number of years, you come home, and you meet with your investors to find out what kind of returns they've made on your money. The first one hands you $100,000! "What?" you say. "Are you serious? Thank you so much! That is incredible. Wow! The next time I leave I will give you more to manage. I am so happy with you. This fills me with joy. And you should be happy, too, because you have exceeded my expectations."

After similar positive results with the second investor, we skip to the third man, who simply says, "Here is the $10,000 you asked me to take care of for you."

"What?" you are flabbergasted. "Are you kidding me? You didn't buy stocks or bonds or mutual funds, or even put the money in a CD so I could have gained a little interest? Give me that $10,000! I'm giving it to the one who earned me $50,000; I know he will do something of value with it."

There is a profound principle here, my friend. When we invest wisely and devoutly with the talents God has given us, he gives us more. When the servant who buried his money returned the talent he was given, that talent was immediately given to the one who had doubled the master's five talents.

"Therefore take away the talent from him, and give it to the one who has the ten talents. For to everyone who has shall more be given, and he will have an abundance; but from the one who does not have, even what he does have shall be taken away" (Matt. 25:28, 29).

When do we receive our rewards for investing well? Not until heaven? Could it be that we experience rewards from heaven here on earth for our good stewardship of his resources? Just ask some of the people who have been featured in this book. For example, how does Sean Lambert feel each time he witnesses

There is a profound principle here, my friend.
When we invest wisely and devoutly with the
talents God has given us, he gives us more.

a poor Mexican family receiving a key to their brand new home? Or, how does Don Schoendorfer feel when a disabled elderly woman sits in one of his wheelchairs for the first time?

That is joy. It is reward. It is complete fulfillment.

Remember the young man I met for coffee in Texas? He longed to be a senior pastor and, in the process, missed the talents right under his nose: two young men who worked for him, two couples in his Sunday school class. He could have cared less about them. But it's my belief that those were the "talents" God had put in his life for that season.

What had he done with them?

Buried them.

Forgotten about them.

Glossed right over them, with eyes on his own prize—and his own idea of success.

You know what I'd like you to do, if you haven't already? I'd like you to get on your computer and visit some of the inspiring websites I've provided in this little book:

- Homes of Hope
  —www.ywamsdb.org
- Austin Gutwein
  —www.hoopsofhope.org
- Axxess Energy
  —www.communityupliftministries.org
- Westfall Group
  —www.westfallgroup.net
- Opportunity International
  —www.opportunity.org
- Free Wheelchair Mission
  —www.freewheelchairmission.org
- Wycliffe Bible Translators
  —www.wycliffe.org
- Watoto Child Care Ministries
  —www.watoto.com
- Hyatt Moore
  —www.hyattmoore.com
- Cure International
  —www.cure.org

- The Seed Company
  —www.theseedcompany.org

I did so when I was writing this book and it absolutely moved me.

I think it will move you, too.

If nothing else, it will reinforce the message I've tried to impart in this chapter: buried treasure is something none of us should want anything to do with! And let me be the first to tell you, if you have buried your talents, it's not too late to dig them up and put them to work—before the Master returns!

Buried treasure is something none of us should want anything to do with! If you have buried your talents, it's not too late to dig them up and put them to work—before the Master returns!

Discussion Questions

1) Jesus said, "Whoever finds their life will lose it, and whoever loses their life for my sake will find it" (Matt. 10: 39). Discuss the verse and what it means to you as it relates to giving yourself up for God's use.

2) Read and discuss Matthew 24: 45-51 as it relates to Jesus' return, what he finds you doing at that time, and what you believe he expects of you.

3) Read Matthew 25: 1-13. Discuss your thoughts about this parable as it relates to Jesus' return. Is he coming back? Is he serious about what he expects you to be doing while he's away? Is Jesus going to reward you when he gets here, or possibly punish you? Are you ready for his return?

4) When we invest wisely and devoutly in the talents God has given us, he gives us more. When the

servant who buried his money returned the one talent he had been given, that talent was immediately given to the one who had doubled the Master's five talents. Discuss your thoughts about receiving rewards for investing well. Does it happen now? Not until heaven? Both?

9

WHERE THERE'S A TREASURE, THERE'S A TEST

Finding your sweet spot in this thing called life

When I stand before God at the end of my life, I would hope that I would not have a single bit of talent left, and could say, 'I used everything you gave me.'

— Erma Bombeck

I know of a distinguished businessman in Detroit who, along with his wife, was growing in the faith and determined that God wanted him and his wife to entrust part of their treasure to him. They decided that, for one year, they would give ten percent of their income to God's work. After doing so successfully, they were prompted to give an additional one percent

*When I give financially or hear of others who do so
with heartfelt generosity, I only learn remarkable
stories of how lives are blessed, talents are multiplied,
and joy overflows.*

the next year, and an additional one percent each year thereafter.

Based on the eternal truths in the parable of the talents, what do you guess happened to that couple?

If you guessed they stopped giving when they reached fifteen percent a year, you're wrong. In fact, they reaped so much good fruit and abounding joy from their endeavor that they upped the ante. The last I heard, the couple was giving away more than seventy percent of their annual income.

I can just picture God laughing as he cries out, "'Test me now in this,' says the Lord of hosts, 'if I will not open for you the windows of heaven, and pour out for you a blessing until it overflows'" (Mal. 3:10b).

Have you ever known anyone who has given sacrificially and ended up in want? I have not. In fact, the opposite is true. When I give financially or hear of others who do so with heartfelt generosity, I only learn remarkable stories of how lives are blessed, talents are multiplied, and joy overflows.

Friends of mine, Stan and Kay, are some of the most generous people I know. When Stan and I were playing golf recently, the conversation turned to a matter near and dear to both of our hearts—high-quality, high-impact, mission-minded organizations. I began to probe to find out more about what made Stan and Kay tick, to get to the bottom of what made them so generous, and to find out more about their philosophy of stewardship.

"As you consider the resources God's entrusted to you," I said, "how do you develop a plan to be a good steward?"

In his ever-gracious manner, with his tender southern drawl, Stan looked at me and said, "Bob, Kay and I don't want to be good stewards . . . we want to be *great* stewards."

I've never forgotten that statement.

I often think of it when I teach about the parable of the talents. As I mentioned earlier in the book, the word "talent" spoken of in the parable is a measure of weight and actually means "money."

It's been said, "When God gives you a financial windfall, it is not only a blessing, but a test!" Indeed, I believe the "talent" of treasure is probably one of the most difficult to steward.

A vital truth I have learned in recent years is this: God gives us passions for a reason. It's not his style to drop thousands of dollars fluttering out of the sky. He uses his people as conduits through which to bless others. That's really the crux of the matter, isn't it?

The Bible says, "Where your treasure is, there your heart will be also" (Matt. 6:21). Where is your heart? You very well may find the answer to that question as you discover the "talents" God has entrusted to you.

If you've looked at any of the websites of the organizations mentioned in this book, I'm sure it has confirmed to you that we live in a hurting world. The Free Wheelchair Mission site shows a video of men, women, and children dragging themselves through the dirt streets of Third World countries. The Cure International site shows poor, hungry, diseased people in need of food, water, medical assistance, shelter, and compassion.

The earth's labor pains have resulted in massive earthquakes, typhoons, floods, and tsunamis, resulting in shortages of homes, food, clothes, and love. If we will take the time to look, we will see a world in desperate need.

What is my responsibility?

What is yours?

How can we help? Do we have the ability?

Exactly what abilities has God given you?

What should we give in the form of our time, talents, and treasures?

Don't get stressed about it.

Don't give hurriedly out of some knee-jerk, legalistic obligation.

Don't give with the motive of gaining riches in return from a god you picture as some kind of cosmic slot machine.

And don't give with the motive of gaining riches in return from a god you picture as some kind of cosmic slot machine.

This book is all about getting in stride with your maker.

Tuning in to his heart.

Finding out what you were created to do and be and give.

That's what life is about—losing your life, finding God's plan.

Remember, there's no one else like you. No one in this whole world has your ability, passion, talent, desire, and, perhaps, money. The key for you is to zero in on the specific talents God has left in your hands— right under your nose—and to invest those talents wisely and faithfully.

Remember, "God loves a cheerful giver" (2 Cor. 9: 7b).

Once you begin to faithfully steward the talents he's entrusted to you, brace yourself.

For the joy is coming.

And I can promise you, it will blow away every concept of joy you've ever entertained in the past.

Jesus put it this way: "By this my Father is glorified, that you bear much fruit, and so prove to be my disciples. . . . These things I have spoken to you, that *my joy may be in you,* and that *your joy may be made full*" (John 15:8, 11 ESV, emphasis mine).

Discussion Questions

1) Have you ever known anyone who has given sacrificially and ended up in want, or the opposite? Discuss.

2) The Bible says, "Where your treasure is, there will your heart be also" (Matt. 6: 21). Be honest—where is your treasure today? What do you value above all else? Are there any "heart" changes you need to make? Pray about those.

3) We live in a self-centered society. It's easy to get caught up in ourselves, our families, and our own little worlds. But there are a lot of desperate people out there. According to the Bible, what is your responsibility? Do you have the ability to help—where? What should you give in the form of your time, talents, and treasures? Discuss.

4) Jesus said: "By this is My Father glorified, that you bear much fruit, and so prove to be my disciples. . . . These things I have spoken to you, that My joy may be in you, and that your joy may be made full" (John 15: 8, 11). How do you bear much fruit for God? Read John 15: 4-6 and discuss.

THE PARABLE
OF THE TALENTS

For it is just like a man about to go on a journey, who called his own slaves and entrusted his possessions to them. To one he gave five talents, to another, two, and to another, one, each according to his own ability; and he went on his journey.

Immediately the one who had received the five talents went and traded with them, and gained five more talents. In the same manner the one who had received the two talents gained two more. But he who received the one talent went away, and dug a hole in the ground and hid his master's money.

Now after a long time the master of those slaves came and settled accounts with them.

The one who had received the five talents came up and brought five more talents, saying, 'Master, you entrusted five talents to me. See, I have gained five more talents. His master said to him, 'Well done, good and faithful slave; You were faithful with a few things, I will put you in charge of many things; enter into the joy of your master.'

Also the one who had received the two talents came up and said, 'Master, you entrusted two talents to me. See, I have gained two more talents.' His master said to him, 'Well done, good and faithful slave. You were faithful with a few things, I will put you in charge of many things; enter into the joy of your master.'

And the one also who had received the one talent came up and said, 'Master, I knew you to be a hard man, reaping where you did not sow and gathering where you scattered no seed. And I was afraid, and went away and hid your talent in the ground. See, you have what is yours.' But his master answered and said to him, 'You wicked, lazy slave, you knew that I reap where I did not sow and gather where I scattered no seed. Then you ought to have put my money in the bank, and on my arrival I would have received my money back with interest.

Therefore take away the talent from him, and give it to the one who has the ten talents.' For to everyone who has, more shall be given, and he will have an abundance; but from the one who does not have, even what he does have shall be taken away. Throw out the worthless slave into the outer darkness; in that place there will be weeping and gnashing of teeth.—Matthew 25: 14-30